IMAGES
of America

VENICE
CALIFORNIA

Dedication

I humbly dedicate this small book to Kendrick Kinney, son of Innes and Helen Kinney and grandson of Abbot and Margaret Kinney. He is a self-made man who began life without the privileges of money or position. Kendrick excelled in the motion picture industry, working at M.G.M. on classic films such as *The Wizard of Oz* and *Gone With the Wind.* He is the Academy Award-nominated sound editor for *The Wreck of the Mary Deere.* Mr. Kinney's career was a very distinguished one.

I met this man and his charming wife Barbara at the beginning of my first Venice book project. Without his knowledge and influence, many doors to Venice secrets would have remained closed to me. His recommendation to the Michel family was directly responsible for the second Venice book I wrote, concerning Herman Michel. Kendrick's support and confidence regarding all of my Venice history projects has been unwavering. Mr. Kinney, I fondly salute you!

IMAGES
of America

VENICE
CALIFORNIA

Carolyn Elayne Alexander
Presented by Venice Historical Society

ARCADIA
PUBLISHING

Published by Arcadia Publishing
Charleston, South Carolina

Library of Congress Catalog Card Number: 99066659

For all general information contact Arcadia Publishing at:
Telephone 843-853-2070
Fax 843-853-0044
E-Mail sales@arcadiapublishing.com
For customer service and orders:
Toll-Free 1-888-313-2665

Visit us on the Internet at www.arcadiapublishing.com

CONTENTS

ACKNOWLEDGMENTS

This book could not have been written without the aid and cooperation of so many people. Foremost among them are Jack and Mary Kinney, who owned the scrapbooks of amateur photographer Thornton Kinney, Abbot's eldest son. Sadly, both of these fine people are now deceased.

Members of the Venice Historical Society and its board of governors have embraced my idea for this work and provided information, photos, and family records. You will read their names in the courtesy line at the end of captions.

Likewise, Venetian residents and former residents have taken an interest in my work and contributed interviews and pictures. Without their combined perspective, this book would have no form or meaning.

Dr. Arthur Verge opened up a whole new aspect of Venice to me when he spoke to Venice Historical Society in November of 1998 on the history of lifeguarding. Since that time, his straightforward generosity and willingness to give of his time and resources has added immensely to both our archive and our understanding of the guards, and the sports of swimming and water polo.

The master photographer Herman Hartzel of Hartzel Studio is responsible for the sterling clarity of many images in Sandcastles. Mr. Hartzel has given of his own time in retouching pictures for this book. Any less-than-perfect images used herein are my doing. He generously donated photos and increased my knowledge of the area, as only someone who has been operating a camera since the 1920s could have accomplished.

Many thanks to Schell Alexander for his assistance in locating 1970s, 1980s, and 1990s photographs and his suggestions for chapter titles in this book.

Tom Anderson, Venice High School Alumni Association archivist, and the board of directors of that fine group, have been most giving of their photos and very interesting files. They responded to my cries for old yearbooks and Gondolier newsletters, giving me a concept of their school that I could have never otherwise gained.

Many libraries and societies have helped in the collection of photos seen herein. Notable among them is Carolyn Kozo Cole of the Los Angeles Public Library. Also, Lucille Cappas, head librarian of the Abbot Kinney Memorial Branch, Los Angeles Public Library, has always shared with me whatever history has passed over her desk.

Michael Steen and his assistants, Phyllis and Millie, at Woodlawn Cemetery have been most forthcoming with their files, broadening my understanding of local families and providing clues as to where I might look for descendants to interview.

Last but not least, I thank Art Palmer for serving as my back-up editor. His command of punctuation far exceeds my own, and we had many battles over commas.

Images seen in this book without a courtesy acknowledgment are property of the author. Should anyone reading this book be a member of a pioneer family of Venice, I would welcome an e-mail or telephone call from you: SHELANE@AOL.COM or (310) 967-5170.

Introduction

If New Jerseyan Abbot Kinney had not been born with asthma, Venice, California, would never have been built. In 1850 there were few treatments for this condition so when government lawyer Franklin Kinney and his Virginia socialite wife, Mary Cogswell, realized tiny red-haired Abbot had a problem, little could be done to help him.

He was a brilliant child, so much so that he alone of all the siblings was sent abroad for education, after a sojourn at Columbia University. The University of Heidelberg, the Sorbonne in Paris, and various schools in Switzerland honed and broadened his intellectual curiosity. Abbot interested himself in science, writing, botany, and especially languages. When he finally returned to the States, he spoke seven foreign tongues. President Ulysses S. Grant hired him to translate a Civil War history written in French.

In his mid-20s, he formed a partnership with his brother Francis, in Kinney Brothers Tobacco Company, a tremendously profitable venture. Because of his celerity with languages, he was the self-appointed foreign buyer. Some of his tobacco buying trips spanned three years and he resided more in the east than he did in the land of his birth. He returned from one such long foray in 1880, when his ship docked in San Francisco. Foremost on his mind was training southeast to Florida and a fashionable health spa, to find relief for his debilitating asthma.

Mother Nature, in all of her measureless wisdom, placed a cumbersome snowfall in the High Sierra Mountains just prior to Kinney's departure, and he was persuaded by acquaintances to journey south instead, to Southern California.

Disembarking in the small village of Los Angeles, Abbot was appalled by the distasteful atmosphere near River Station. Wooden sewer pipes were crushed in numerous places and their contents mixed with ever-present mud, as hoof beats from many horses churned the elements together. He located a conveyance to drive him to what is now East Pasadena, and set off as rapidly as possible, to escape the powerful stench of "The City of Angels."

The Sierra Madre Villa Hotel was a well-known hotel/sanitarium, and they were without a vacancy when the easterner inquired for a room. Always hospitable however, they arranged a comfortable pallet on the billiard table for their exhausted guest. He later declared that evening to be the most restful he had ever spent.

It wasn't long before he located a piece of sale property, owned by a hermit beekeeper, which sat on what Kinney considered an ideal bluff. He constructed a large white frame house overlooking the valley, where he could see all the way to the ocean. A reservoir was dredged, out buildings were assembled, and Kinney hired a retinue of Chinese workers to develop *Kinneloa* (meaning Kinney's Mountain in Hawaiian). With botany as an abiding interest, he developed new strains of fruit but became well known throughout the state for the blood oranges produced at Kinneloa.

After the passage of three years and a failed bid for the California State Legislature, Abbot met and married pretty Margaret, the daughter of State Supreme Court Justice William Dabney Thornton. However, the inland summer climate of Kinneloa was not suited to Margaret's well being, so a home at Ocean Avenue and Marguerita in Santa Monica was constructed for the hot months. She christened it Mayflower Cottage.

In this approximate time frame, Kinney sold his shares in the tobacco company back to brother Francis. It is not known how much he received from the sale but we can comfortably assume the amount was considerable.

Abbot began land speculating in Los Angeles with the proceeds from his tobacco shares. Among other investments, he owned the Abbotsford Inn and inaugurated the Boyle Heights Cable Railway. A man of many accomplishments, he founded libraries, wrote numerous books, and was the chairman on a Yosemite Committee. Kinney also accompanied Helen Hunt Jackson as translator and friend when she made her trip to Indian country, to report on appalling living conditions to the government. Her book, *Ramona*, arose out of that effort.

The move to the shores of Santa Monica Bay occasioned his meeting with Francis Ryan and the formation of a land development partnership that was the primary step in the building of Venice. The two men purchased Rancho La Ballona where they built a walk/fishing pier in the Ocean Park section of Santa Monica, developed a commercial street, a family entertainment casino, and a bandstand. Kinney arranged for the train from Los Angeles to make regular stops at the pier. They were off and running.

The hamlet of Ocean Park would have been Abbot's life work if Ryan had not suddenly passed away in the Fall of 1898. Within six months, his helpless widow married again, and her new husband did not like his partner's methods. T.H. Dudley sold Matilda Ryan's 50 percent share to four men, with whom Kinney also could not agree.

Abbot suggested tossing a coin to see which 50 percent of the property would be his and which half would belong to the others. The four men assented and the coin was tossed. Kinney won, but instead of choosing the developed half of the Ocean Park property, he selected the southern salty marshland. His partners were amazed but very happy not to have lost their considerable investment.

In May of 1904, the *Santa Monica Outlook* newspaper carried a description of Kinney's elaborate scheme for a cultural renaissance on the sandy shores of the Pacific Ocean: a "veritable Coney Island." The local residents laughed with derision and someone nicknamed it Kinney's Folly.

Although the area was called Venice, it was really a part of the Ocean Park district of Santa Monica until 1911, when residents voted to break away from the mother town and become an independent city.

Through the photo captions in this book, read the fascinating story of Venice-of-America, her golden years, her decline, and the upward surge as the new millennium commences.

A 1930s Venice beauty poses on the beach in a bathing costume of two decades past. (Courtesy Bison Archives.)

One

PRELUDE TO A LEGEND

Red-haired Abbot Kinney was born in 1850 at Brookside Farm, Morristown, New Jersey. Shown second from left, at age 20, he is playing chess with another young male student while studying abroad at Heidelberg University in Germany. Always a brilliant student, he spoke seven languages when he returned to the United States. (Courtesy Lee and Kent Kinney.)

Pictured here is the Sierra Madre Villa Hotel, since demolished, in the district now called East Pasadena, California. It was in this hilly health spa/hotel that Kinney first found relief from his lifelong asthma in 1880.

Kinneloa Ranch was constructed in 1881 on land formerly owned by a hermit beekeeper. Although Abbot Kinney grew many edibles on his property, he became well known for his blood oranges. (Courtesy Jeremy Kinney.)

Blue-eyed Abbot Kinney, age 34 in 1884, is seen here on the occasion of his marriage to Miss Margaret Dabney Thornton. Kinney was rarely seen without a flower in his lapel and a straw hat on his red hair. (Courtesy Kendrick Kinney.)

Margaret Dabney Thornton and her father, State Supreme Court Justice James Thornton, were residents of San Francisco. Maggie was well known for her singing, which graced many social gatherings. (Courtesy Kendrick Kinney.)

Shown here are the walk and fishing pier constructed by partners Francis G. Ryan and Abbot Kinney. If Ryan had not passed away at an early age, Ocean Park would have been Kinney's life work. (Courtesy Getty Center for Art and Humanities.)

Ocean Park Pier at Pier Avenue is pictured here, c. 1903. The bandshell provided classical music for a Los Angeles public that was hungry for entertainment. The casino was a restaurant and family amusement center.

14

The digging and dredging the Venice-of-America canal system in 1904 is pictured here. Far center is Kinney's Lagoon Bath House, and to the left is the beginning of Venice's main street, Windward Avenue. (Courtesy Kinney Family.)

Windward Avenue is shown here under construction, as seen from the roof of the Venice Bank Building at the corner of Trolleyway (now Pacific Avenue). The iron colonnade was set in place before the brick structures were built around them.

Pier lumber arrived aboard a boat in late 1904. Kinney set his July 4, 1905 grand opening date for Venice-of-America. Local residents laughed and dubbed it Kinney's Folly.

Pier pilings, tarred for waterproofing, were to be used in the T-shaped pier adjoining Windward Avenue. Workers lived in the surrounding suburban areas. (Courtesy Kinney Family.)

16

In keeping with Kinney's plans for a cultural renaissance, the Auditorium was the main feature of the pier. When Abbot began Venice-of-America, he requested government permission to build the first private breakwater. (Courtesy Kinney Family.)

On March 13, 1905, a storm wiped out most of the pier, Auditorium, and Ship Hotel. With the grand opening date of July less than four months away, Kinney hired 600 workers to labor around the clock. The following day, the permission letter for the breakwater arrived. (Courtesy Kinney Family.)

The second T-shaped Abbot Kinney Pier and Auditorium is shown here under construction. The top of the T was used to dump rocks from Chatsworth, California, to form a breakwater. Locals began to believe in Kinney's plans and visited the half-finished pier to check on progress. At right is the unfinished Ship Hotel. (Courtesy Kinney Family.)

Two local ladies sat on the beach in front of the newly completed St. Mark Hotel at Windward and Ocean Front Walk (the Broad Walk). A marble lobby, staircase, and an elevator gave prestige to the hotel, later featured in a 1950s movie. (Courtesy Gloria Canelli Saluto.)

Two

THE LEGEND IS BORN

On July 4, 1905, Venice-of-America opened to an influx of some 40,000 curious visitors, an enormous turn-out considering the small population of Los Angeles County. Real estate was sold that day totaling $405,000. (Courtesy Kendrick Kinney.)

Patriotic concerts featuring 400 voices with the 42-piece Venice-of-America Band, art exhibits, water basketball, swimming races, fancy diving exhibitions by Jake Cox, dancing at the Auditorium, and an elaborate display of Japanese fireworks over the graceful Grand Lagoon, made up the exciting opening day agenda. (Courtesy Kinney Family.)

The Venice Miniature Railway was commissioned by Abbot Kinney to show prospective real estate purchasers various parcels of land for sale in the little canal city. Three engines were ready to pull a set of open-air cars around a three-mile circuit. (Courtesy Kendrick Kinney.)

The Miniature Railroad stands outside the car barn at what is now the corner of Abbot Kinney and Venice Boulevards. Innes and Carlton Kinney, sons of the founder, were the chief officers of the company. Not shown is the white-frame roundhouse and the brick ticket station. (Courtesy Jackie Gerety Konrad.)

Strollers pass the new pavilion at the land end of the pier. Fashion of the day dictated that a lady's skin be milk white, so female beach-goers wore long sleeves and high necks, not to mention large hats. Swimming was dangerous at a beach without regular lifeguards. (Courtesy Kendrick Kinney.)

Dry grocers Reed and Young stand in their Market Street establishment, which was deemed by them, "a model of cleanliness." Italian immigrant Cesare Menotti owned the first green grocery in town, located on Windward Avenue in the heart of the commercial district.

Crowds gather for an aquatic event on the Grand Lagoon in 1906. From left is the Lagoon Bath House, the Antler Hotel, the diving platform, Midway Plaisance, and the Amphitheater, where band concerts were performed twice daily. (Courtesy California Historical Society.)

Visitors at the Lagoon Bath House and crowds below await a water performance on the Grand Lagoon, while the Boat House and Midway Plaisance come to a standstill in anticipation. The round cement object in the center foreground was used to launch elaborate fireworks shows.

The spacious Amphitheater had not yet filled as the swimming races commenced at the Grand Lagoon. Honors such as ribbon-hung medals were given as prizes for the winning of aquatic events. Later in the evening, the large Amphitheater was used to seat viewers at the Japanese fireworks shows. (Courtesy Los Angeles Public Library, Security Pacific Photo Collection.)

The Midway Plaisance opened in 1906 with a bevy of odd buildings and even stranger performers. The Streets of Cairo (Egyptian exhibit), Darkness and Dawn (fun house), Temple of Mirth (fun house), Madame Fatima (belly dancer), The Igorots (Filipino headhunters), and Bosco Eats Them Alive (reptiles) were among the features. (Courtesy Seaver Center.)

The Trained Wild Animal Arena was situated between Fair Japan, a Japanese Theater and Exposition, and The Streets of Cairo, a replica of the Algazara Plaza. Early in its history, the Egyptian exhibit caught fire, but the only damage to the interior was the waterlogged mummies. (Courtesy Seaver Center.)

Madam Chiquita, a 30-inch-tall South American, rode a diminutive bicycle and danced at the Midway Plaisance in Venice. Here, she is shown comparing her height to that of a giant, over 8 feet tall, and an average size man, 5 feet 9 inches tall.

Innes, third son of Abbot Kinney, shakes hands with Chief Chy-Anne of the Filipino headhunters. When the tribe was told that its tenure on the Midway was over, the proud chief applied to the city trustees for a job as Venice dogcatcher. He said, "You no pay me, just give me dogs." He did not get the position. (Courtesy Kendrick Kinney.)

Koko, the Midway's main barker, stands at the entrance to the Midway, next to the Venice Miniature Railway, megaphone in hand. To his left is Gaston Akoun, the show's promoter. Glitzy as the appeal was, the show only thrived for four years. The public tired of the camels, the performers, and their unique surroundings and clamored for something new.

Across from the Midway was an idyllic scene just east of the confluence of Lion and Grand Canals. In the background on the right is Villa City with cottages with canvas sides, constructed so that the poor could afford accommodations in Venice-of-America. (Courtesy Kinney Family.)

The rail spur, used to haul rocks for the breakwater, was also appropriated to bring the private railcar of Sarah Bernhardt to the Pier Auditorium. The Kinney Co. was anxious to please the grand dame of the stage, so when she tried her luck fishing from her dressing room window, they hired boys to swim out and hook fish to her line.

Not many souvenirs were mass-produced in the early part of the 20th century. In 1907, French-born Madame LeFevre and her son Achille hand sewed exquisite lacy handkerchiefs and offered the service of embroidering the name or initials of the purchaser while she waited.

The 1908 Life Saving Corps were the only guards on the beach until Captain George Douglas Freeth, right, made a daring rescue when five Japanese fishing boats and their 11 occupants were trapped in raging seas. The Hawaiian was credited with saving six people and received a Congressional Medal of Honor. Abbot Kinney saw what was needed, and professional lifeguarding was born.

Children's dancing lessons were held inside the Pier Auditorium with the help of a live orchestra to play music for the young students. It was a marvelous opportunity for Venice mothers to visit and gossip with other local ladies of the burgeoning little community.

An oriental exposition on Abbot Kinney Pier exhibited a heritage not familiar to either Southern Californians or the many visitors beginning to flock to the unusual town from all over the world. Kimono-clad representatives, pagodas, paper lanterns, and a carved red dragon curled around the gateway all welcomed the bemused viewers. (Courtesy L.A. Public Library.)

Inside the Japanese exposition, salespeople sold an amazing variety of imported goods such as china, silks, jade jewelry, statuettes, and dolls. Curious Angelenos fingered the items tentatively and bought generously. Some of these items are still in the possession of local families.

Strollers on Ocean Front Walk view the (then) narrow beach and homes of the wealthy as they walk toward the amusement district at Windward Avenue. On the right is the brand new, enormous, warm salt water Plunge building constructed in 1910 over the Surf Bathing Pool.

The beach was narrowing due to an improperly constructed breakwater. Particularly in winter, sand was carried out in the bay but then returned in three or four months. It was not unusual for the high tide to wash under homes on Ocean Front Walk.

The Sells Brothers Circus wintered in Venice for many years, and their largest elephants were used to test the strength of one of Abbot Kinney's arched bridges in this unusual publicity stunt. The ornate spans were all designed by Italian metal sculptor Felix Peano. (Courtesy Jackie Gerety Konrad.)

Six miles of graceful canals intersected streets in Venice-of-America. Fairy-like, multi-colored light globes lined the banks of these waterways with colorful names such as Aldebaran, Coral, Lion, Venus, Cabrillo, Altair, and Grand Canals. (Courtesy Los Angeles City Archives.)

An unknown lady and her baby daughter are poled over Venice Canals in a gondola with red velvet upholstery. Early gondoliers sang to their patrons, and some were actually brought from Venice, Italy, to perform the task. Because of the early century prejudices against minorities, Caucasians were permitted to ride in any of the watercrafts, while African Americans were restricted to boats painted black. (Courtesy Shades of L.A. Archives, Los Angeles Public Library.)

A boat-like fish stand called "Venice" vends freshly caught seafood to pier sojourners. The world-famous Orange Julius was invented in Venice, and it is also rumored that the hamburger was first served on the early Abbot Kinney Pier. (Courtesy Los Angeles Public Library.)

Manfredi Chiaffarelli, center, led the Venice-of-America Band in the Pavilion. He and his family were brought from Italy specifically to fill this city post, but after his 14-year-old daughter, Wilhelmina, was tragically killed in 1914, he resigned and accepted another orchestra leader's position in Santa Monica. (Courtesy Sonya Reese Davis.)

In a typical posture, Mrs. Harry C. Mayer and her daughter Sarah Louise pose in 1910 at an Ocean Front Walk photo studio. This background scene was painted to resemble the early Abbot Kinney Pier with the Ship Hotel on the left and the Auditorium on the right. (Courtesy Michael Jager.)

In a slightly different view of the same scene, musician Pietro Canelli and his soprano wife, the former Aida Barilotti, mug for the big camera in oversized yellow straw fishing hats. Note the two realistic painted, wooden fish at their feet. (Courtesy Gloria Canelli Saluto.)

The country club at Westminster and Trolleyway was the scene of a number of tennis tournaments. Early women's champion May Sutton Bundy won titles here as well as Abbot Kinney, the California men's singles champion. The Doge of Venice was an avid exercise advocate who swam in the ocean every morning. (Courtesy Kendrick Kinney.)

In 1911, Miller's Ford dealership was erected at the rear of the Bank of Italy on Trolleyway near Windward. An employee was storing a 15-foot snake inside the building, which escaped into sewer lines, terrorizing tenants of businesses for two blocks in all directions. The python was finally captured and turned over to its owner with the admonition that he find a new home for his dangerous pet. (Courtesy Merrill Miller and Betty Miller Tomeo.)

Margaret Thornton Kinney is shown, *c.* 1911, with an unknown friend posing in a rolling chair, the earliest form of public transportation on Ocean Front Walk. She passed away from complications relating to diabetes not long after the picture was taken. A Christian Science funeral was held for her in Woodlawn Cemetery, Santa Monica. (Courtesy Kendrick Kinney.)

Jake Cox, Plunge manager and local movie stuntman, donned a fuzzy suit, doused himself with kerosene, and fired off a gun, the spark igniting his suit. He then dove from the rafters of the Plunge into the pool beneath as a publicity ploy to bring patrons to the establishment. When the public tired of his act, he persuaded a pilot at the Venice Flying Field to take him up over the ocean at night. With the panache of a D'Artagnan, he repeated the thrilling feat for the mesmerized crowd lining Ocean Front Walk. (Courtesy Kendrick Kinney.)

The Cadillac Hotel, built in 1914, still stands at the corner of Ocean Front Walk and Dudley Avenue. Originally a honeymoon hotel renting rooms for as little as $1, it fell on hard times like the rest of Venice late in the 1940s and became a popular rooming house for elderly Jewish immigrants. It underwent extensive remodeling in the 1980s and is once more a well-patronized hostelry.

To provide a constructive summer environment for area youth, Venice Military Academy was founded in 1914 by Colonel William Strover of the U.S. Army. The boys were domiciled at the country club, which afforded a series of wide open spaces where they could exercise and be drilled in marching. They were fed hearty meals and a lot of discipline during the hot months of that year.

Strong bones and well-developed muscles were two of the goals of the institution. Some of the 6 to 15-year-old boys came from Venice's working-class families, while others were born of wealthy Santa Monicans. All of the young "soldiers" were provided with a handsome military-style uniform and a shiny new weapon, for which they cared and displayed proudly.

Young men from the Venice Military Academy enjoy a warm day's outing on the Grand Lagoon in a luxurious gondola. Rowboats were provided for their physical education classes by Abbot Kinney so that the boys might develop upper-body strength. The institution only existed for one summer because it was not a financial success.

Abbot Kinney remarried in 1914 to London-born Winifred Harwell, a former dental student from the University of Southern California. The Doge remodeled the former Cosmos Club for ladies into a larger, more stylish home, and the couple moved into their new dwelling at One Grand Canal facing the Grand Lagoon. (Courtesy Jackie Gerety Konrad.)

Two children were born to Abbot and Winifred Harwell Kinney. Helen grew up to be a laughing, lighthearted woman who married Jack Gerety, the son of Venice's mayor. The youngest, Clan, was always regarded as a moody, eccentric man. He was briefly married to an Al G. Barnes Circus elephant rider named Patricia Clancy. (Courtesy Jackie Gerety Konrad.)

The Abbot Kinney Bath House was remodeled into a high school in 1911, but soon after, property was purchased on Venice Boulevard to build a much finer brick structure. Groundbreaking ceremonies were held October 28, 1914, at Venice Union Polytechnic High School. Less than two months later, the Bath House was destroyed by fire. (Courtesy Venice High School Alumni Association.)

In 1917, Cesare LaMonica took up the baton for the Venice Band, whose members were Italian immigrants. LaMonica was a well-known and loved musician in the Santa Monica Bay district, but when World War I was declared, he was arrested as a "slacker." He explained that he had not known about enlistment and immediately volunteered. (Courtesy Gloria Canelli Saluto.)

VIEW ON THE CANAL, VENICE, CALIF.

Constructed on Coral Canal, the Venice Union Church was led by Reverend Fenwicke L. Holmes. He was ably assisted by his brother, Earnest Holmes, who later founded the Church of Religious Science along with Mabel Cohen, who became the wife of Thornton Kinney, Abbot's eldest child.

A popcorn and candy vendor stands near the head of the Abbot Kinney Pier with his wife in 1918. Most snack food items sold for 5¢, while large hot dogs and thick hamburgers were priced at 10¢. Coffee was 5¢ with free refills in most restaurants.

Central School in Venice, later called Westminster, was one of three grammar schools. The total student population of the city in 1910 was 1,000 with 31 teachers. The total value of all of the school properties was $135,000.

Broadway School, also called Abraham Lincoln, is pictured here, c. 1919. An unknown teacher supervises sliders during recess in this typical American scene. Cathryn Peasgood, daughter of James T. and Lou Vera Cady Peasgood, stands at the far right with a bow in her hair. (Courtesy Ken McCracken.)

George D. Fieg stands at his strength-testing concession at the ocean end of the Abbot Kinney Pier. The Venice Wireless Station (radio and telegraph) is at his left. The Aquarium, which was also the U.S.C. Marine Biological Research Station run by Innes Kinney, is at his right.

Duke Kahanamoku, famous swimmer, a descendant from Hawaiian royalty, stands beside a very heavy redwood surfboard emblazoned with his name. Duke and George Freeth were Hawaiian aquatic marvels who performed in Southern California since the early years of the century. (Courtesy Kinney Family.)

The beauty contest began in Venice as a newspaper promotional stunt in 1912 and was always the most popular event, attracting a large visitor turnout. Many of the contestants were aspiring silent movie actresses, and others were established stars hoping for publicity for their films. The events reached a peak in the 1930s and 1940s when Miss California competitions were held in the Venice Pier Auditorium. (Courtesy Adelbert Bartlett.)

Venice girls spoof a train robbery at the Miniature Railway, *c.* 1917. Bathing wear was in transition, going from pantaloons to woolen tank suits. Famous swimmer Annette Kellerman was arrested on the beach for abandoning the law-required stockings. Mayor Gerety went to court and declared he "would not like to swim while wearing socks," so the law was overturned. (Courtesy Venice High School Alumni Association.)

Built on the site of demolished Midway Plaisance, the Race Through the Clouds roller coaster was constructed in 1911 and thrilled visitors to Venice until 1925. With the strains of a little calliope playing, two cars raced side-by-side on the wooden track, providing an element of chance to the outcome of the ride. Owner Thomas Prior was forced to roll a peanut with his nose from the 'coaster to the pier when he lost a bet. (Courtesy Los Angeles Public Library.)

Graceful Aldebaran Canal moves quietly past flower-enshrouded banks. The canal waters were controlled by the rising and falling of tides, flushing the waterways. Tidal gates controlled the salty brine after storms and occasionally had to be dynamited when they became jammed with silt. Much of Venice was at or below sea level. (Courtesy Kinney Family.)

The Short Line Railroad built a canal system in 1905 in South Venice, smaller but similar to Kinney's. Lila Everett poses before diving into the 4-foot-deep waters, c. 1919, while the occupant of a nearby canoe watches with interest. The Grand Canal, which intersected Kinney's system, ran the whole way to the sea. (Courtesy Los Angeles Public Library.)

Abbot Kinney, right, pauses to watch the filming of a silent picture on the Pier, c. 1917. The name of this movie was possibly *Tom and Jerry Mix*, starring Tom Mix. Venice has always been a popular site for the making of motion pictures. (Courtesy Jackie Gerety Konrad.)

Otto Meyerhoffer was sworn in as the country's first flying policeman by Mayor A.E. Coles in 1918 at the Venice Flying Field. The main focus of his job was to chase speeders and scan the Pacific Ocean from his aerial view to report swimmers in trouble. Not too many years later, he was killed stunting in another aircraft off the Venice Pier.

30,350. In Thrift Stamps
Sold in 11 Days.
This amount will do any one of the following:
BUY 400,000 Bullets.
7500 Hospital Beds.
Buy bread for 7500 Soldiers for 1 Month.
Will feed 15,000 Soldiers for One Day.
Buy 7500 Gas Masks.
Furnish Monthly Allowance for 1000 Soldiers' Families.

HELP WIN THE WAR
BUY THRIFT STAMPS HERE and FULFILL YOUR PLEDGE

We Sell 20 Paddles at 25¢ Each and Give to the Holder of the Paddle, Numbered the Same as the Disk drawn from the Box, $5.00 in THRIFT STAMPS. No Profit to Anyone Connected with the Sale. EVERY PENNY RECEIVED GOES TO THE GOVERNMENT. This is the First Thrift Stamp Paddle Game Booth started in the United States. Our Success has started Hundreds all over the Country and Millions of Dollars are Now being Raised for the Government by This Plan.

HELP WIN THE WAR—BUY A PADDLE

World War I broke out, and all of Venice mobilized in some way for it. The Prior twins raised pigeons for the army, food staples were rationed, a store owner placed a box to collect used tin foil at his entrance, and a grocer named Menotti asked for old string. Thrift stamps were sold to Venetians, and silent film stars like Mary Pickford and Douglas Fairbanks appeared in many public places to raise money for the war effort. (Courtesy U.S.C. Special Collections.)

49

Abbot Kinney was just short of his 70th birthday in November 1920, when he was diagnosed as terminally ill with lung cancer. With his family at his side, he slipped into a coma and slept into death. He was a man of unique personality, a quiet egalitarian with a magnetic personality. He was a gentleman of vast attainment and a philanthropic human being who championed the poor and loved children. His town mourned his passing. (Courtesy Jackie Gerety Konrad.)

Only one month later, Venice was dealt a second tragedy. A heater in the Dance Hall burst into flames and quickly took the entire building with it. The blaze spread on the large wooden Pier as merchants ran for their lives, carrying armloads of kewpie dolls, cash registers, live turkeys (given as prizes in one game), and anything else they could carry.

VENICE PIER FIRE DISASTER

Water from both the Plunge and the Pacific was used to fight the fire, but the Abbot Kinney Pier was not coated with creosote and burned to the water line at low tide by dawn. The Plunge was saved. The Kinney family was in shock. The pier was not insured, and their father had left his money in a 12-year, unbreakable trust fund.

Fire Chief Herbert Harlan, who was awarded his position for the successful disarming of a trolley hold-up man, was the only fatality of the conflagration. After fighting flames from the roof of the Ocean Inn when it partially collapsed, he was thought to be recovering from his serious burns when he suddenly succumbed to shock.

Parts of two rides near the land end of the pier were saved as were buildings on the oceanfront, but the fire ranked as the worst on Santa Monica Bay. Christmas was bleak. A dance floor was laid in the Plunge for the annual New Year's Eve celebration. Merchants, town residents, and the Kinney family feigned merriment and determination to hide distress. An era was ended.

Three

CONSOLIDATION
AND DECLINE

Thornton Kinney was heir to his father's trust-bound company, and he had no access to the money he needed to rebuild the pier. Borrowing on the family's good name, he accepted the task, and reconstruction began only one month following the devastating conflagration. On July 4, 1921, a newer and better pier rose from the ashes. (Courtesy Los Angeles Public Library.)

Lawrence Furniss was the architect of the commodious new Ballroom. It was outfitted with velvet-covered furniture and tapestry hangings, not to be surpassed by the magnificent marble bathrooms. Dances were 10¢ or a dollar for a book of one dozen tickets. Loges were provided for parties, and an upstairs viewing gallery was free to all. (Courtesy David Furniss.)

The new Venice Pier was a hedonist's paradise with racing cars, a giant fun house, Noah's Ark (which was used in Charlie Chaplin's movie, *The Circus*), wooden horse racing, games of chance, concerts, a new Ship Cafe, side shows with duo-sexed people, enormously obese twins, sibling Swiss midgets, a reptile man, Ossified Roy (a stone man), and all else imaginable.

The Race Through the Clouds, east at the Lagoon, was still attracting a large crowd, while the Giant Dipper provided thrills at the entrance to the pier. Another coaster at the sea end of the pier made riders feel as if they were plunging into the water. The Little Rascals filmed a movie called *Fish Hooky* that featured the sea end coaster. (Courtesy Los Angeles Public Library.)

Everyone's favorite ride on the Venice Pier was the Dragon Slide, which involved riding around in a burlap sack inside the dragon's body until emerging on the pier, 99 feet down. Painful bamboo splinters were a frequent complaint. Alber's Waffle Parlor (also featuring flapjacks) is shown at left, and the Chocolate Garden, in the Ballroom, is on the right.

Ocean Front Walk was lined with merchants in 1920, many of them selling food items. A new electric tram ran between Ocean Park and Venice. Note the tired lady towing her baby carriage at the rear of that wicker and canvas vehicle. (Courtesy Ruth Wallin.)

Captain Henry W. Behrens, a professional diver, ran an undersea diving concession called the Pirate Ship. A glass plate in a tank separated the viewer from the diver, and in 1913, the glass fractured. One minute the diver was in water, and the next, he was in open air. Luckily the water disappeared between large slats in the floor. (Courtesy Betty Speer.)

56

Red-haired Amelia Florence Behrens was Captain Behrens's daughter and favorite protégé. Air was cranked through a hose to the diver during the 1920s. During one descent, Amelia almost passed out when the cranking Italian employee, having had garlic for lunch, leaned too close to the air supply while turning the wooden handle. (Courtesy David Furniss.)

Amelia Miller Behrens (Mrs. Henry Behrens), center, founded the Venice Baby Bank on the old pier and carried the business over to the new structure. Small babies were kept in numerous cribs, and after their departure, a new length of sheet pulled off a roller while the soiled part dropped into a basket. Patrons exchanged tots for a brass claim check. (Courtesy Betty Speer.)

57

In lieu of a sandwich board, this tall figure strode down Ocean Front Walk advertising the Fun House. Owned by Walter D. Newcomb, its interior held a rolling barrel, assorted sliding boards, a revolving dish electrified in the center, and a small coaster. Air jets blew women's skirts. The original Bozo the Clown worked here. (Courtesy Los Angeles Public Library.)

Fishing was encouraged on the pier, and old photos show the enormous size of some breeds before contamination eliminated them from Santa Monica Bay. In the center background, the Flying Trains (airplanes on mechanical arms) are seen. Elderly residents remember that each unit was controlled by the rider and that it felt as if one was flying free of the mechanism.

Californians have always worshiped health and beauty. Handsome lifeguards, well-developed muscle men, and would-be silent film actors gather for a male beauty contest just north of the Venice Pier. There was obviously no age limit judging between the two widely disparate figures on the right. The youngster's sign reads, "Grandpa Prefers ME!" (Courtesy Elliot Welsh.)

Children's beauty contests were embraced with an immense amount of enthusiasm by parents in Venice and the neighboring district of Ocean Park. Some kiddies dressed in costumes, while others just wore their best Sunday dress. (Courtesy Los Angeles Public Library.)

Contestants for the pageants turned out in droves. Little girls were taught to pout and vamp like silent film stars of the 1920s, and elaborate costumes were ingeniously stitched by their loving mothers for the beauty competitions. Note the sultry Mae West attitude on the saucy child to the left. These three girls were winners c. 1921. (Courtesy Los Angeles Public Library.)

The city of Venice's first prize-winning float in the Pasadena Rose Parade of 1922 was designed by Harry Winebrenner of Venice High School. It was entitled The Spirit of Venice and featured a kelp-covered float with a wave breaking over the queen of the sea, student Miss Myrna Williams, later to be called Myrna Loy in the movies. (Courtesy Tournament House.)

The Peasgoods were typical Venetians: J.T. Sr. and wife Ellen, plus city treasurer James Jr., his daughter Cathryn, and his sister Clara. In a corrupt city government, where young Jim was pressured to keep up with the lifestyles of other officials, he "borrowed" small amounts of money that reached $18,000. He was sent to prison but released after one year and pardoned by the governor. Jim led an exemplary life afterward. (Courtesy Ken McCracken.)

Mr. and Mrs. James T. Peasgood Sr., solid and upstanding citizens, prepared to take leave of their home on Electric Avenue. He was the street superintendent of the City of Santa Monica and is shown here with his second wife, Ellen. The house still stands in the 1600 block of Electric Avenue in Venice. (Courtesy Ken McCracken.)

Stunts gave Venice the publicity she needed to keep bringing crowds who spent money at the beach. Here, girls rode blocks of ice that were towed behind new car models, probably advertising the cars. Checking closely, the reader can see a piece of rug on which they are seated. (Courtesy Los Angeles Public Library.)

A game of giant checkers is played on the beach by women in swimsuits with trophies hovering in the background for the winner and loser. This event did not attract much attention unless the watchers were situated out of view. (Courtesy Los Angeles Public Library.)

A Most Beautiful Back Contest as well as Beautiful Red-Head, Blonde, Brunette, etc. brought a large influx of males to the city. Because of the lure of the movie industry, it was said that the most beautiful people in the world lived in Southern California. (Courtesy Betty Speer.)

Children participate in the lighting of a faux firecracker to advertise the coming of a Fourth of July celebration on the Venice Pier, c. 1926. Holidays were observed with a great deal of fanfare, especially New Year's Eve and Independence Day. (Courtesy Adelbert Bartlet.)

An auto park was added to the large pier to accommodate the many cars coming to Venice. The dilemma of where to put vehicles had become critical, and the Kinney Company tried to alleviate the problem with their addition. (Courtesy Los Angeles Public Library.)

Harry Winebrenner, Venice High School Art Department Head, sculpts the "welcome" statue that stood at the apex of Grand Lagoon until it was filled in 1929. During filling, the piece was bumped by machinery and toppled into the dirt where it stayed. The Lagoon area was paved over and made into a traffic circle, which it remains to the present. (Courtesy Los Angeles Public Library.)

This image shows Venice versus a Los Angeles Athletic Club team in a game of water polo at the Grand Lagoon in the 1920s. Wool swimwear lacking undergarments make it readily apparent, when the tango was sweeping the nation, why a law was passed to prohibit the dance from the beach. (Courtesy Bison Archives.)

The Red Arrow Bonded Messenger Service utilized motorcyclists (Bob Murdock, second from left) for fast delivery of packages and telegrams. Located on Lincoln Boulevard, they played a prominent role in communication when not everyone owned a telephone. (Courtesy Robert Murdock.)

The earliest tram running between Ocean Park and Venice could be piloted from either end of the conveyance. Tony Kinney, head of the Kinney Company, paid the female driver 10¢ fare on this 1920s postcard. The rider next to him giggled behind a white-gloved hand.

United States Island was called St. Mark when Abbot Kinney dredged the canals, but it was developed in 1912 by a man who named each bungalow after a state. In the courtyard stood a large model of the United States Capitol. Most of the cottages still stand in Venice along with the lamppost seen in the center. This postcard was produced in the 1920s.

Venice City Hall, left, was constructed in 1906, and because residents were angry that it was so far away from town center, they said it was "far away as Tokio [*sic*]" and nicknamed it "Tokio City Hall." On the right is the 1920s police station with a prisoner dropoff point at the portico. (Courtesy Milton Slade.)

Six Santa Monica Bay piers are pictured here. They are, from the background moving to the foreground, as follows: Santa Monica, Bristol, Ocean Park/Lick, Venice, and Sunset (angled.) The empty spot on the Venice Pier was clear for the parking of automobiles. The Ship Cafe was turned south when the new pier was still on the drawing board.

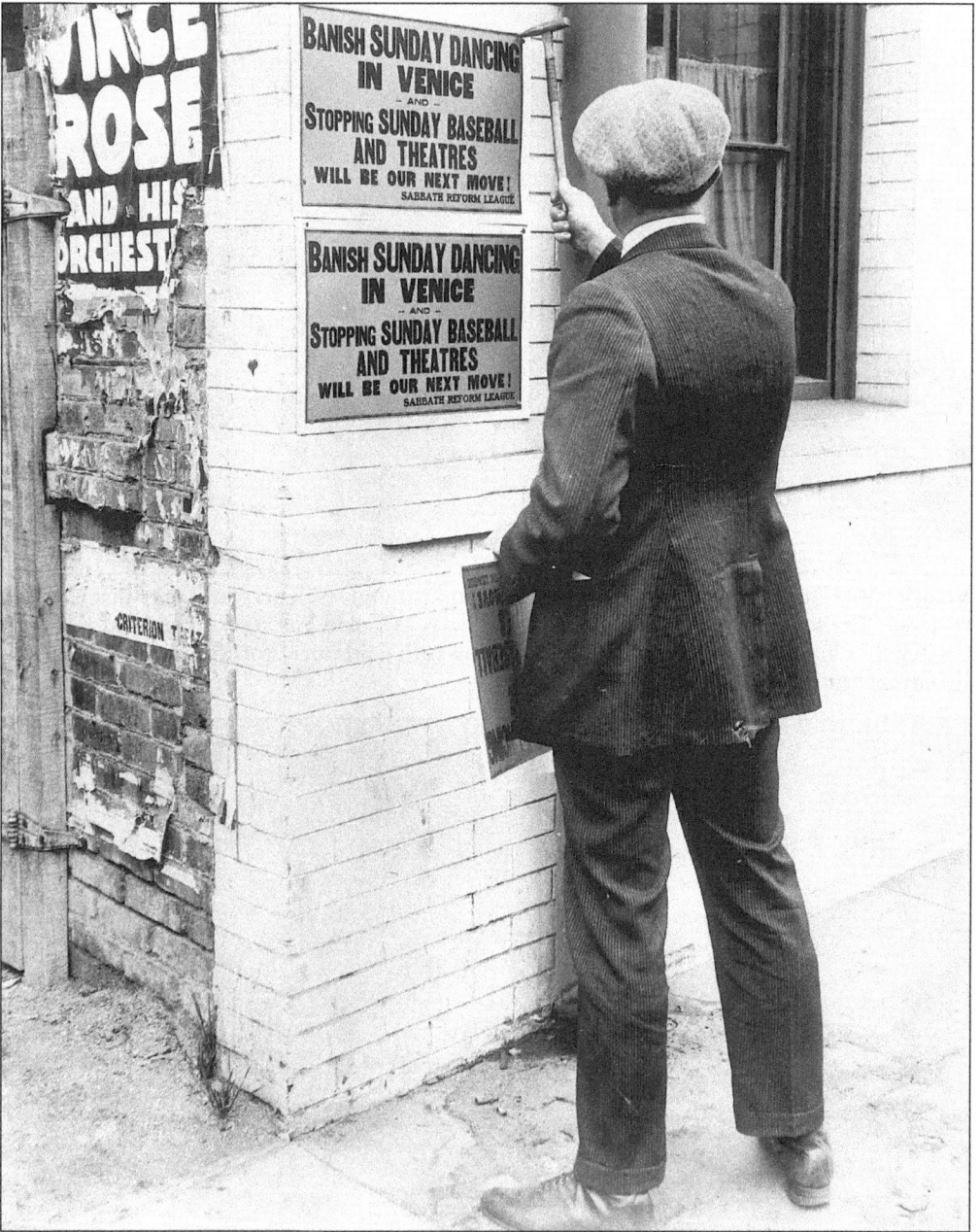

The Sabbath Reform League became very active in Venice at the request of some local religious institutions. Sunday dancing was prohibited for a period of time, but the pier and Ocean Front Walk merchants complained that their receipts were affected by the Blue Laws, and they were eventually overturned. (Courtesy Los Angeles Public Library.)

Because of the narrow beach, the sand became very crowded most summer days. Umbrellas rented for six hours at 50¢. An ex-beachboy said that he learned a lot about life retrieving those umbrellas. The Waldorf Hotel, the large white building to the left, was scaled in 1919, without benefit of climbing apparatus, by Jack Morris, the Human Fly. (Courtesy Elliott Welsh.)

Venice High School girls celebrated Mayday, c. 1924. Beatrice Owens, front row, right, later won the title of Miss Ocean Park and went on to a career in the final days of vaudeville on the Orpheum Circuit, on stage, and in the movies. (Courtesy Beatrice O. Dilworth.)

Two tiny chums wear rented bathing suits from the Venice Plunge. The concept of bacteria was different in the 1920s than it is at present. The suits were worn in both the Plunge and on the beach, washed in a commercial-sized tub, and hung on the roof of the structure to dry. One summer, over 500 suits were stolen, and after that, patrons were searched when departing.

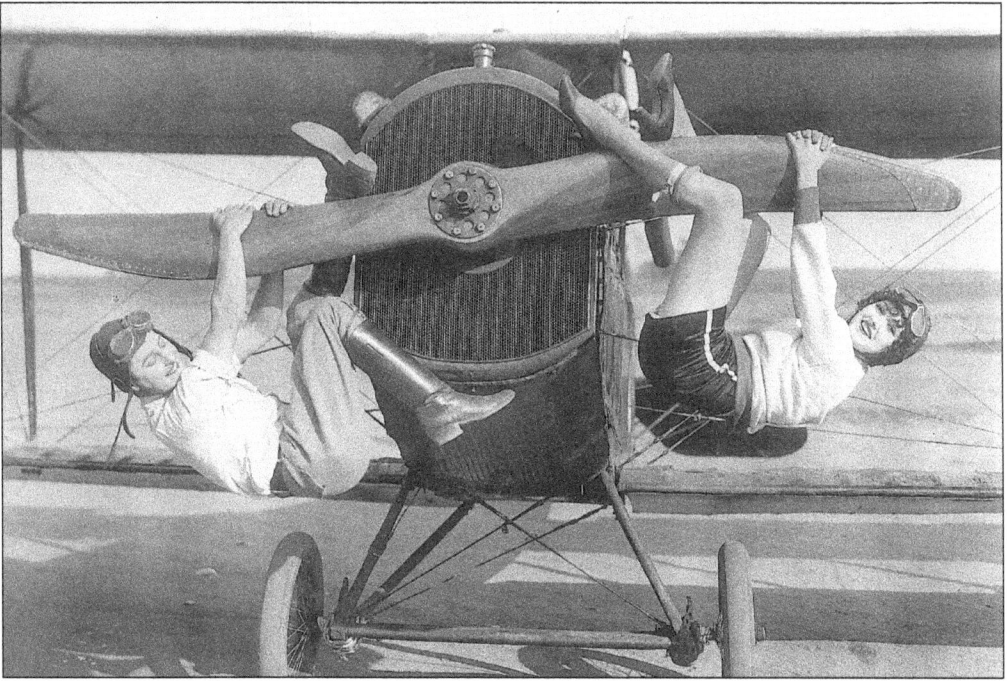

The Venice Flying Field spawned a whole new industry in Hollywood when stunting aviators, hired to perform over the town, made the airport their home. Frank Clarke, Frank Tomick, and Al Wilson, shown here in a publicity still from an unknown movie, thrilled crowds of visitors with their plane-to-plane transfers and other daring feats. (Courtesy Venice Historical Society.)

Thomas H. Ince, fourth from left, was a silent movie producer who purchased the Flying Field and named it after himself. He was successful in business but sold the property after only four years. Not two years later he was fatally shot aboard the *Oneida*, William Randolph Hearst's yacht. The case was never solved. (Courtesy Bison Archives.)

As a commercial venture, the Kinneys purchased a plane for hauling passengers, but the business never quite prospered. Donald Douglas, already building his own aviation empire, and Helen Kinney are seated in the rear of the Cloudster cockpit. (Courtesy Jackie Gerety Konrad.)

Windward Avenue had progressed at an astonishing rate due to the hordes of visitors to the city. But it was not enough. Taxes were at state-regulated maximum. The canals were jammed with silt, and low tide increased the odor of rotting fish. The town still could not pay their bills. Consolidation with Los Angeles was the only answer, or so they thought. Voters confirmed consolidation in 1925.

After Venice consolidated with the City of Los Angeles, real troubles began. A new fire engine was removed, and an old rattletrap from downtown L.A. replaced it. The Miniature Railway and its tracks were removed as a hazard to traffic. (Courtesy U.S.C. Special Collections.)

The worst blow to the city came when Los Angeles took the deed between Abbot Kinney and Venice to State Superior Court. The document gave the canals to the city "to be held as public waterways forever." The court overturned the stipulation and granted Los Angeles the right to fill in Kinney's canal system, so there would be more thoroughfares to bring traffic to the pier.

Paralyzing floods swept the city after a series of unusually severe winter storms, and Venice Boulevard, the main artery leading from Los Angeles to Venice, was inundated with water. The hourly Pacific Electric train could not bring visitors to the pier until the driving rains had stopped and the deep flood receded. (Courtesy Venice Historical Society.)

The Southern Canal district, unfilled because it was not a part of Kinney's gift to the city, was below sea level and flooded with much of the rest of the city. A large dog, left behind by accident when his owners evacuated their home, howled all night in fear until rescuers in a rowboat came to reunite him with his worried family. (Courtesy Venice Historical Society.)

74

To make matters worse, the Ohio Oil Company discovered oil on the southern peninsula of Venice, and derricks appeared overnight like mushrooms. Soon, it was the state's fourth largest oil field. The City of Los Angeles put few environmental restrictions on the drilling procedure, and the Grand Canal, leading from the southern canals to the sea, was awash with oil.

The beaches always had their problems. Oil, even before drilling, mixed with the foamy waves and washed ashore onto the beach, which had to be closed to swimmers intermittently through the years. Part of the town was permeated with an unpleasant stench. Business on the oceanfront and at the pier fell off. (Courtesy Herman Hartzel, Hartzel Studio.)

The Brooks Avenue Lifeguard Station had been built in 1927, and it quickly developed into a mecca for swimmers and celebrities. Johnny Weissmuller (Tarzan of the movies), Buster Crabbe (another Tarzan), Duke Kahanamoku (surfer/swimmer), Charlie Chaplin (silent film comedian), and Andy Devine (of western movies) were not strangers to the station.

Los Angeles Municipal lifeguards line up for an inspection outside the Brooks Avenue Station in the 1930s. Some guards also worked in the Plunge and at various locations around Los Angeles County. The young men kneeling in dark swimsuits are junior lifeguards. (Courtesy Los Angles Public Library.)

A Los Angeles Municipal lifeguard teaches a small girl the proper strokes of successful swimming. Demonstrations of lifesaving technique were also displayed periodically by these dedicated young men, and the exhibits attracted sizable crowds of ladies. (Courtesy Venice Historical Society.)

Pooches of varied lineal descents are groomed by girls in uniform swimwear for an annual dog show on the beach behind the Plunge. The current Miss Venice, front row, second from left, calms a particularly nervous dachshund. (Courtesy Los Angeles Public Library.)

The Santa Monica Dairy, also called Edgemar Farms, was founded by a Swiss immigrant, Herman Michel, in 1880. The creamery progressed from horse-drawn milk carts to trucks and later to vans before the sons gave up the Rose Avenue establishment in the 1960s. Michel also served as the mayor of Santa Monica about the time this photo was shot. (Courtesy Walter J. Michel.)

Modern equipment was always the standard at Edgemar Farms, and this employee washes bottles in a large-scale machine, placing them carefully in wooden crates after they are dry. Milk was delivered to individual doors in the early days, and in some cases, milkmen put the containers right into customers' refrigerators. (Courtesy Walter J. Michel.)

Publicity stunts were more necessary than ever to boost visitor attendance in the town. These young women race horse-headed cycles down Ocean Front Walk. At left are the new pergolas (called pagodas in Venice), a Work Projects Administration project created by President Roosevelt to assist a depression-blighted nation. (Courtesy Los Angeles Public Library.)

These six young ladies pose for the newspaper at the finish of a coal mine ride on the pier. The two at left on the sleepy-looking burro must have considered themselves very daring to show the tops of their silk stockings, much less ride astride in a skirt for the photograph. All had bobbed hair in the fashion of the 1920s. (Courtesy Los Angeles Public Library.)

Another Miss Venice poses at the top of a ladder while her companions hang large bells on the community Christmas tree. Abbot Kinney made a tradition out of his holiday celebrations, and Christmas was the most awaited. An enormous kiddie party was always held in the Venice Pier Ballroom with a show, free candy, fruit, and a gift for every child. Kinney, who played Santa Claus each year, always said that he would rather have 100 presents left over than be one short. (Courtesy Los Angeles Public Library.)

In the Spring of 1933, the great Long Beach earthquake struck an unsuspecting Venice in the early hours of the morning. The 18-year-old brick high school came tumbling down. Luckily, the large tremor occurred before students were in class, and no one was hurt. (Courtesy Elliott Welsh.)

Another "earthquake" struck the Venice entertainment area. Gambling was illegal in Los Angeles County, but bingo and tango were usually allowed if the right officials received their due. (Courtesy U.C.L.A. Special Collections.)

Another type of "gambling," the promotional kind, took place on the beach when some Miss Venice beauty contestants posed with giant cards in a mock game of poker. The "chips" strongly resemble paper plates and the dog appears to be a part of the "pot." (Courtesy Los Angeles Public Library.)

Miss Venice contestants line up on the stage of the Ballroom for preliminary try-outs. In the early days of the contest, winners were chosen by the amount of applause from the crowd. By the 1930s, professional judges made the decision. (Courtesy U.C.L.A. Special Collections.)

Shown here is the musically famous Lennon family: Bert, a show business agent, and his wife, Betty, a former ballerina. The children were all successful in life, and the boy on the left, Bill, was the father of the Lennon Sisters. Fame took a high toll on them when a mentally deranged fan shot Bill to death at a Marina del Rey golf course. (Courtesy Marietta Lennon.)

Another well-known local family was that of Arthur Reese, the first African American to live and work in Venice. Reese came to town from the New Orleans area in 1905 and observed that the town needed a janitorial service. Another custodian, who decided Venice was his territory, pulled a gun but shot himself in the leg, leaving the job solely to Reese. (Courtesy Sonya Reese Davis.)

When Reese realized the scope of work available, he invited his cousins, the Tabors, to move to the little town by the Pacific. Reese built a house in the new Oakwood section of town and helped the Tabors build there, too. Irving Tabor became Kinney's chauffeur and lived with the family until the Doge died. Irving inherited Kinney's house. (Courtesy Navalette Tabor Bailey.)

It was not long until Reese, an artist and sculptor, began making suggestions to Kinney. In record time, he was named town decorator. This fabulous design was the Ballroom decor for a Fourth of July Ball. He built windmills, snow scenes with chalets, floats for parades, and his own home, and once hung the whole downtown in fresh grapes. (Courtesy Sonya Reese Davis.)

84

Reese soon garnered a large crew of workers who fabricated his designs and painted the floats and hung his ornaments. It was an unusual position for a black man in the early part of the 20th century. Venice became the town it was, principally because of two men: Kinney and Reese, who never called each other anything but Mister. (Courtesy Sonya Reese Davis.)

Arthur Reese came up with the idea to simulate the Mardi Gras in Venice. To that end, he created giant heads from papier-mâché, modeled to resemble celebrities of the time. The famous Venice Mardi Gras was emblematic of Reese's sterling career. Here, one of Reese's employees painted the head of the well-known Esquire man. (Courtesy Sonya Reese Davis.)

The Esquire man posed on the beach with two California lovelies, aspiring motion picture starlets. Reese won a plethora of awards and many honors; however, he was well known as a family man. He and his wife, Gertrude, raised two sons, Lloyd and Mercier. (Courtesy Sonya Reese Davis.)

Intent bathing beauties, in suits less modest than their forerunners, pose with another of Reese's fabricated carnival heads for a chamber of commerce photograph on the Venice Pier. In the background is the South Venice oceanfront. (Courtesy Los Angeles Public Library.)

The Mardi Gras always began with a parade. In this 1932 shot, the fourth vehicle from the right is the King and Queen's float. Queen Venezia was chosen by the sale of buttons bearing her name, and King Neptune, always masked until the Grand Ball, was a local businessman. The most famous of Venice's royalty was William Harrah, yet to found his gambling empire in Lake Tahoe, and his wife-to-be. (Courtesy Los Angeles Public Library.)

The Secret Five functioned similarly to the Keystone Kops in that they incarcerated visitors and merchants who came to the Mardi Gras without benefit of costumes. Venetians wanted to ride in their unique vehicle, so they deliberately schemed to be arrested by this group of black-hooded local businessmen. (Courtesy Los Angeles Public Library.)

Keystone Kops mingled with the costumed crowd in downtown Venice and arrested any visitor or resident found without a disguise. The guilty party was taken before a kangaroo court, fined $2 or $3, and if they could not or would not pay, the court sentenced them to the stocks. Revelry was the key word. (Courtesy Sonya Reese Davis.)

Town merchants and residents alike joined in the preparations for the summer celebration. The Fun House employees are shown here in vehicles used on the pier. The car is from the Racem concession with the manager's son, Wayne Allison, in the driver's seat. Bozo the Clown stands behind him holding an umbrella festooned with balloons. (Courtesy Wayne Allison.)

The Miss California Contest took on new prominence when it became a part of the Venice Mardi Gras. Entrants posed on the beach, the pier, and once even on the wing of an airplane for eager photographers. Motion picture and television star Yvonne DeCarlo got her start in one of the Mardi Gras beauty competitions. (Courtesy Sonya Reese Davis.)

This image shows a Miss California Contest featuring contestants and several fake palm trees atop a specially built ramp on the Venice Pier. The girl third from right was one of the runners-up. Everyone's favorite ride, the Dragon Bamboo Slide, is visible in the background. (Courtesy Herman Hartzel, Hartzel Studio.)

Beauty contest participants discuss their lesser awards and show off trophies in this photograph taken during a Miss California Contest in the 1930s on the Venice Pier. Note how Number 2, in the center, cradles her award like a baby. (Courtesy Herman Hartzel, Hartzel Studio.)

Another judging venue was built on the Venice Pier with the judge's box at the extreme right side of the photo. Two boys are sitting on the wide railing. The Sunset Pier is left of the center in back, and oil derricks can be seen dotting the right rear landscape. (Courtesy Los Angeles Public Library.)

Flanked by two runners-up, the victor holds her large trophy and an even larger bouquet of fresh flowers. (Courtesy Herman Hartzel, Hartzel Studio.)

The culmination of the Mardi Gras was the Grand Ball in the Pier Ballroom, where Queen Venezia was crowned by King Neptune. Note the lavish velvet draperies, double-eagle thrones, and crowns, another Arthur Reese achievement. (Courtesy Los Angeles Public Library.)

The Mardi Gras was later represented with an Arthur Reese float in Pasadena's world-famous Rose Parade. Bo Peep sits amidst greenery on the front, a Spanish lady is seen in the center, and a female pirate and a gaucho appear near the clown's arms. (Courtesy Tournament House.)

Pier business was picking up due to publicity. The mighty arms of the Flying Circus swing out with self-controlled airplanes on the north side of the Venice Pier. Stuntman Jake Cox once jumped from one of the planes for a motion picture. (Courtesy Los Angeles Public Library.)

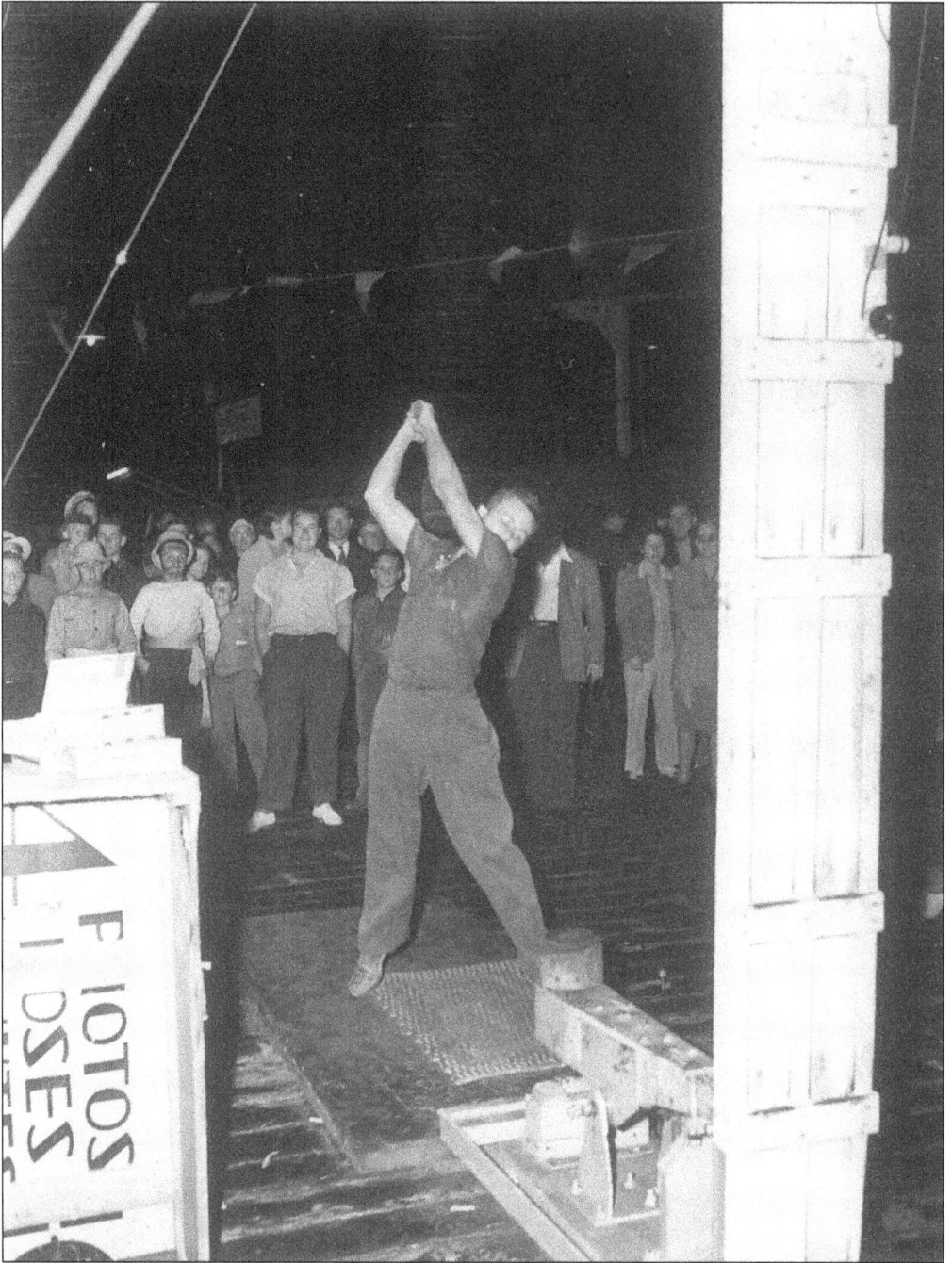

A young man tries his luck in a strength-testing game on the Venice Pier in the mid-1930s. If he could smash the hammer down hard enough on the wooden block, a "bullet" would be propelled to the top of the vertical slide and strike a bell. The prize for such a feat was his choice of a stuffed animal for his date or favorite girl. (Courtesy U.C.L.A. Special Collections.)

Venice boys, practicing water polo every day at the Plunge, were deemed good enough to represent the United States in the 1936 Olympics. Represented by the Los Angeles Athletic Club, the athletes sailed to Germany for games known thereafter as Hitler's Nazi Olympics. (Courtesy Herb Wildman.)

Although the Venetians did not win, they gave a very good accounting of themselves. One team member shared that they all disliked Hitler, who sat in his special box throughout the entire event. They were forced to shake hands with him and receive a fancily illuminated certificate. (Courtesy Herb Wildman.)

Famous Olympian swimmer Buster Crabbe traveled to Germany with the Olympic Water Polo team and was a personal friend of several members. Crabbe should be remembered for his role as Tarzan of the Apes in bygone motion pictures. (Courtesy Herb Wildman.)

The advent of the 1940s saw little change in Venice economy. Things were still sliding. Needed repairs to the colonnades and the streets were not made. The Kinney Company was not clearing enough profit to upgrade the pier, and a group of lawyers had stepped in to control what was left. The most viable business on the pier was the Ballroom with its exhausting dance marathons.

The southern canal banks were crumbling into the waterways and, in places, the sidewalks were sliding after them. Gone were the tri-colored globe lamps and the colorful flowers lining the banks. Neighborhood boys built homemade rafts on which to play pirate games. Lots with a home cost $3,000, and minimum wage was $16 per week. (Courtesy Wayne Allison.)

Speedboats such as the *Miss Liberty* and the *Miss America* were docked at the foot of the pier and took passengers for rides around the bay. They also ferried visitors to a number of boats anchored off the pier to spend a day or an evening. (Courtesy U.S.C. Special Collections.)

One of the boats was a fishing barge which lay just off the Venice Pier in deep water. In the early days of its anchorage, gigantic fish were caught from the craft. But outfall sewers, usually hidden under piers, polluted the Santa Monica Bay, and the larger species of fish went elsewhere.

Another boat was a Chinese junk called the Ning-Po, where a visitor could satisfy his curiosity about the true nature of oriental sea craft. This young man, feigning pain, was photographed enduring the torture pen, where the guilty party could neither sit nor stand. "X" marks the Venice Pier.

Shown here is the crew and bosun of the historic old Chinese junk, Ning-Po, scourge of the Yellow Sea. Sailing in fancy and voluminous uniforms must have been very difficult, if not impossible.

Pictured here is the ornate stern of the historic smuggling junk, Ning-Po, which was tied up near the Venice Pier. The boat had a shiny black lacquer finish with a writhing gold ornate dragon painted on the side and was a popular sight in Venice in the 1930s.

The Rex was another ship anchored off the Venice Pier. It was three miles out into the bay due to anti-gambling laws in Los Angeles County, but there was a difference of opinion as to where the shoreline was located in the bay. Here, authorities fight to board the Rex and close operations and are held off with fire hoses. After a three-day siege, the crew ran out of food and drinking water and surrendered. (Courtesy U.S.C. Special Collections.)

In the 1930s, fierce storms rolled in from the usually calm Pacific Ocean, wrecking the strand. Powerful breakers smashed the shore with such force that paving and brickwork were uprooted and tossed like matchsticks stuck into sand. (Courtesy U.S.C. Special Collections.)

Up to that point, Windward Avenue had weathered well. The Kinney Company constructed a large Venetian one-story building to use as offices (right), and the St. Mark Hotel (left), though outdated in decor, was still a luxury hostelry. The crowd gathered in this photo for an approaching parade.

A "Guess Your Weight" concession greeted customers to the pier in the 1930s. Prizes were plaster kewpie dolls made by Coast Novelty, which was owned by Robert Murdock. Note the tot being pulled by his mother in the kiddie car that was so popular in that era.

Psychics, fortune-tellers, and other clairvoyant concessionaires were always permitted on the pier, but this middle-aged woman, dressed to the nines, was the first handwriting analyst given a license. Photos of film stars who have been evaluated hang behind this merchant.

A Hollywood film crew shot a small replica train on the beach at Rose and Ocean Front Walk for an unknown movie. The tall white building in the background was the hotel from which Amiee Semple MacPherson, founder of the Foursquare Church, disappeared in the 1920s. Sister Amiee appeared in the desert weeks later claiming kidnapping had occurred. (Courtesy Los Angeles Public Library.)

The Venice Pier, with its tall Dragon Slide, looms up in the background of mist as the lifeguards line up to listen to a talk from their superior. A recent television program concerning modern guards, called *Baywatch*, was filmed on the Santa Monica Bay beaches until production costs rose and the show moved to Australia for shooting. (Courtesy Mike Cronin.)

Leo's Drive-In was located on Lincoln Boulevard and attracted the local youth, who used it as a hang-out. Their colorful menu boasted sandwiches for 20¢ (steak 30¢), soups for 15¢, and a full course chicken or ham dinner for 55¢. A dinner named "fish and shoes" consisted of perch and shoestring potatoes for 50¢. (Courtesy Wayne Allison.)

104

Local Japanese people, who farmed the land around Venice, were a peaceful, family-oriented group at the outbreak of World War II. All oriental faces became the objects of suspicion. Finally, they received a notice to pack up and leave their property. They made the best arrangements they could for their land and vehicles. (Courtesy U.C.L.A. Special Collections.)

On April 25, 1942, they lined up at the corner of Venice and Lincoln Boulevards, and they were told to take only what they could carry. There was no violence. The Japanese-Americans went through a processing station and were sent to internment camps. They were released when the war was over but lost most of what they had owned. It was a black element in the history of the United States.

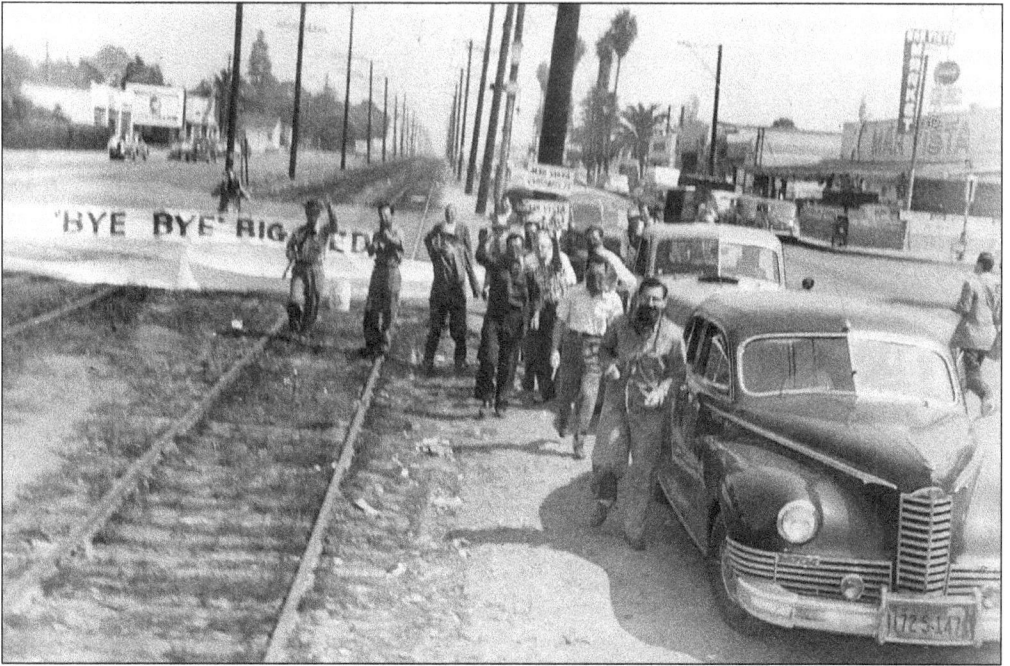

The end of the Pacific Electric Red Cars came about in a relatively sudden way. The Venice Lions Club arranged a goodbye ceremony for the mode of transportation that was a part of everyone's life to date. Here, they greet the train as it leaves Venice to travel through Mar Vista. Buses were scheduled to replace the beloved trolleys. (Courtesy Robert Murdock.)

Business at the pier was sparse, and a more rough, less affluent element began to patronize the concessions that remained open. Revitalizing plans were made, but Thornton was not the businessman his father had been, and there was no cash. (Courtesy Wayne Allison.)

There was a move by the state to tear down piers. The Kinney Company's lease on the tidelands expired in 1946, and the company never envisioned a problem with renewal. When the City of Los Angeles refused to sign a new lease, the Kinneys were outraged. The whole of Venice had belonged to their father, and only through his generosity did the city now own the land. But the city council said tear it down, and so it began. (Courtesy Los Angeles Public Library.)

Some of the rides were sold to amusement parks or other piers, while others were just demolished. The Flying Circus, seen here, was one of the latter. The pier came down slowly, and finally, in 1947, it caught fire. The destruction was complete. Venice's economic base was destroyed. It was the end of the Golden Era. (Courtesy U.S.C. Special Collections.)

Four

THE COUNTERCULTURISTS

After the pier came down, the Plunge and other attractions on the oceanfront were demolished as well. Rents plummeted and drew a poorer class of people. Disillusioned veterans from the Korean War formed a group known as the Beats, and they moved into Venice with a vengeance. Shabby conditions at the southern canals drew the poor to living quarters there.

The Gas House, run by Eric Nord, and the Venice West Cafe, owned by John Haig, became hangouts for this group, who shunned tradition. The Beats wrote poetry, painted, and played their cool jazz. They also slept wherever they could find space, ate on charity, and dedicated themselves to leading lives of creative self-expression. (Courtesy Los Angeles Public Library.)

If nothing else is to be said for the Beat era in Venice, it was the advent of the artistic and literary communities, which still exist today. Beyond, Baroque Literary Foundation is based in the 1906 City Hall. Mural art is recorded by the Social and Public Art Resource Center (SPARC) centered in the old police station. The mural shown was the first in Venice. (Courtesy Leo Bayless.)

Other more sophisticated murals have been painted since the first one, such as this beautiful Windward Avenue building work by Art Mortimer in the 1970s. SPARC gives selective and interesting van-driven art tours.

In Santa Monica, a group of physical culturists assembled an informal group in the 1930s, known as Muscle Beach. Weightlifters and acrobats performed on the beach until the city tired of crowds and prohibited performances in 1958. Some moved to Venice and built a platform in 1950, but they were not an attraction until Muscle Beach closed. (Courtesy Mike Cronin.)

Muscle men worked out on the beach, developing a craze that swept the nation. It was the beginning of the Jack LaLanne movement, which taught the public the importance of exercise and good eating habits. Contests, such as Mr. America, have been held in Venice, and celebrities, like Arnold Schwartzenegger and Hulk Hogan, have lent their support to the cause. (Courtesy Leo Bayless.)

The weight pen attracted visitors from all over the world and more men than women in the early days of its Venice tenure. At left, small bleachers hold a crowd of interested tourists. (Courtesy Mike Cronin.)

The 1980s weight pen revealed more female interest, not only in the male weightlifters but in women developing their own muscles and competing in body culture contests. Today, the viewer can see many feminine lifters working out in the new Muscle Beach building and yard.

In 1952, eight-year-old Mary Sue Bayless, atop the small red caboose, romps at the beach playground across South Ocean Front Walk from her parents' diminutive luncheonette. The sands in Venice are very white. (Courtesy Leo Bayless.)

A nearby neighborhood grocer poses gamely for a photograph in front of his store at the corner of Pacific Avenue (formerly Trolleyway) and North Venice Boulevard (formerly Pico). A typical 1920s building, it now houses a restaurant. (Courtesy Leo Bayless.)

Orson Wells, in dark suit and white open shirt on the right of the car, directs his well-known 1950s movie, *A Touch of Evil*. Wells, the villain, used the run-down Windward Avenue for outdoor scenes and Ocean Front Walk as the border crossing into Mexico. Oil wells and the Grand Canal Bridge afforded a turgid background for Wells's death. (Courtesy Leo Bayless.)

The rundown St. Mark Hotel lobby was used in the film featuring Charleton Heston and Janet Leigh. In less than a decade, a new Los Angeles law, the Earthquake Code Enforcement Act, coerced the demolition of the St. Mark and other hotels. It also caused the removal of upper floors from some buildings and the amputation of all ornamentation. (Courtesy Leo Bayless.)

Advocates for Venice independent cityhood, Larry and Kathy Sullivan, writers at the *Beachhead*, an alternative newspaper, sit on the south beach near the 1960s walking pier off Washington. Dogs were not permitted on the beach, but, for a while, nude bathers prevailed. (Courtesy Kathy Sullivan.)

West of the canals, on the oceanfront, sports abounded. Bronx lovely Jill Prestup, once a candidate for the Los Angeles City Council, concentrated on an approaching ball during a fast game of paddle tennis. Basketball, shuffleboard, gymnastics, and handball are alternatives for beach athletes of varying ages. (Courtesy Jill Prestup.)

Local beauty Maryjane prepared for a day of calm surfing on the canals. Crumbling banks, hordes of ducks, and silt-jammed channels did not detract from the unique beauty of these waterways. Because this was a low rent area, the flower children moved into the cottages in the 1960s bringing love-ins and canal festivals and communes. (Courtesy Rick Sinatra.)

116

The Washington Pier closed for several years until a $10 million bond issue provided monies to refurbish the structure. Schell Alexander gazes pensively toward the wire mesh barrier that prevented joggers from traveling beyond the land end of the pier.

The wheels are rolling, rolling, rolling. Bikers exercised in the cool ocean breezes on the sunny Venice beachfront. There were, and still are, occasional accidents, usually occurring from a speeding rider or the breaking of other rules. The cement bike path circles the entire beach around beautiful Santa Monica Bay. Both strollers and skaters use the path to their peril.

Rollerskating became the rage in the 1970s, when polyurethane wheels were invented. The new wheels were used on skates, skateboards, and even chairs in this revolution. *Time* magazine named Venice "the outdoor rollerskating capital of the world."

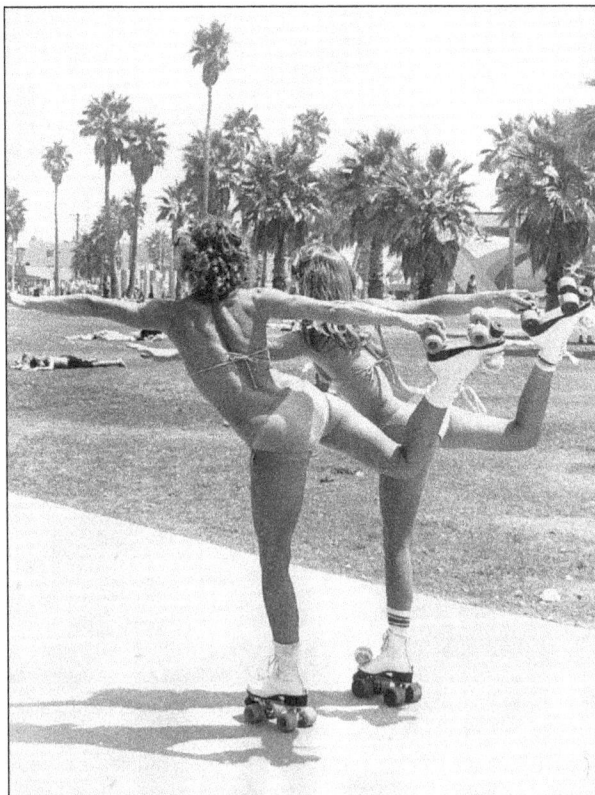

Fancy dancing and acrobatic skating were what brought the tourists back to Venice en masse. They danced alone, in pairs, and as a group. They swerved through obstacle courses and jumped over barriers. A skateboarding grandma once appeared on a national television talk show.

118

Five

THE PHOENIX ARISES

On the strand, crowds from the British Isles, Europe, and Japan flocked to see the carny atmosphere on Ocean Front Walk, or the Boardwalk, as it is called. All kinds of merchandise is sold on the east side of the Walk.

Slated for demolition in the year 2000, the unused 1960s Pavilion will provide a large beach view area to construct a skate park, promised to the denizens of the Venice oceanfront for some years by the City of Los Angeles. Toxic waste, caused by spills from a longtime on-site oil derrick, lies under the Pavilion.

On the west side of the Boardwalk, beach umbrellas shade psychics, face painters, magicians, clowns, massage "doctors," artists, and those with a cause, such as those wanting to legalize marijuana or radical Christian fringe groups. In the background is a new pillared and colonnaded structure erected by Venetian David Dror, a local hero by stringent historical society standards.

Exquisite murals are painted on many old buildings on the east side, such as the structure seen at the corner of Dudley and Ocean Front Walk. Local people gather in the early morning to jog, walk dogs, or breakfast with friends before the crush of tourists arrives for the day.

The Sidewalk Cafe is a longtime friend to most Venetians. It is considered the most beautiful building on the oceanfront because of the preserved pillars, the capitals, and the colonnade under their awning. Bob and Mary Goodfader also run Small World Books in one side of the structure. The Venice Plunge once occupied the space in front of Sidewalk Cafe.

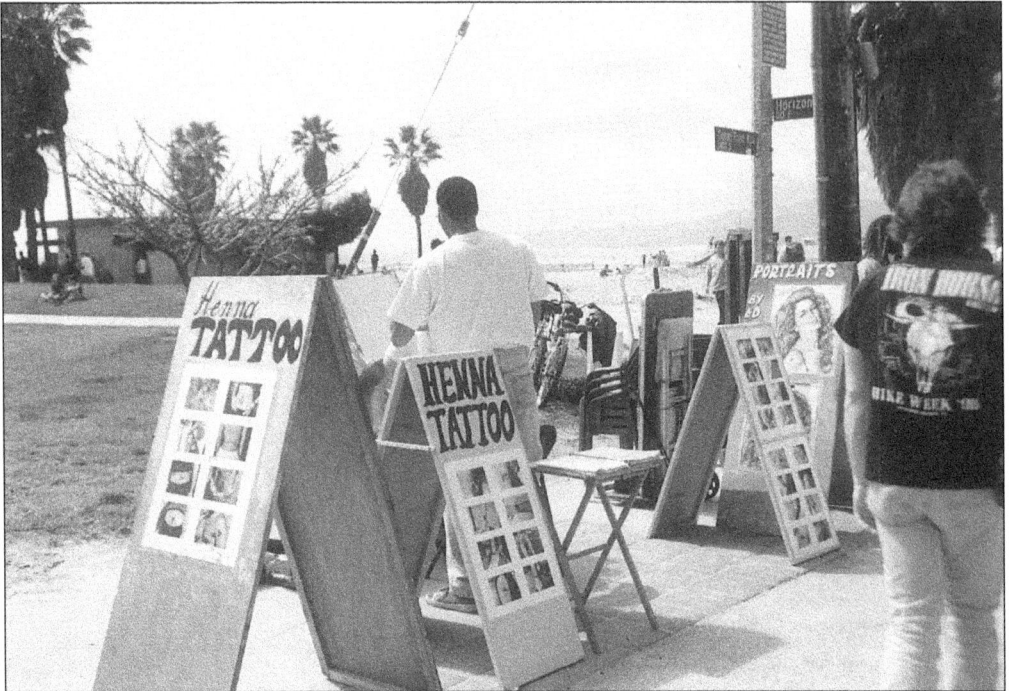

The City of Los Angeles has unsuccessfully attempted to stop unlicensed merchants from occupying the west side of the Walk because their sales interfere with the profits of renters on the opposite side. Nonetheless, the battle continues across Ocean Front Walk.

Community Awareness Day on the Walk features, from left to right, a city-sponsored booth, the Venice Historical Society, and a group campaigning for the rights of dogs. The booths received little attention as the visitors came to Venice to view the weird or the unusual.

122

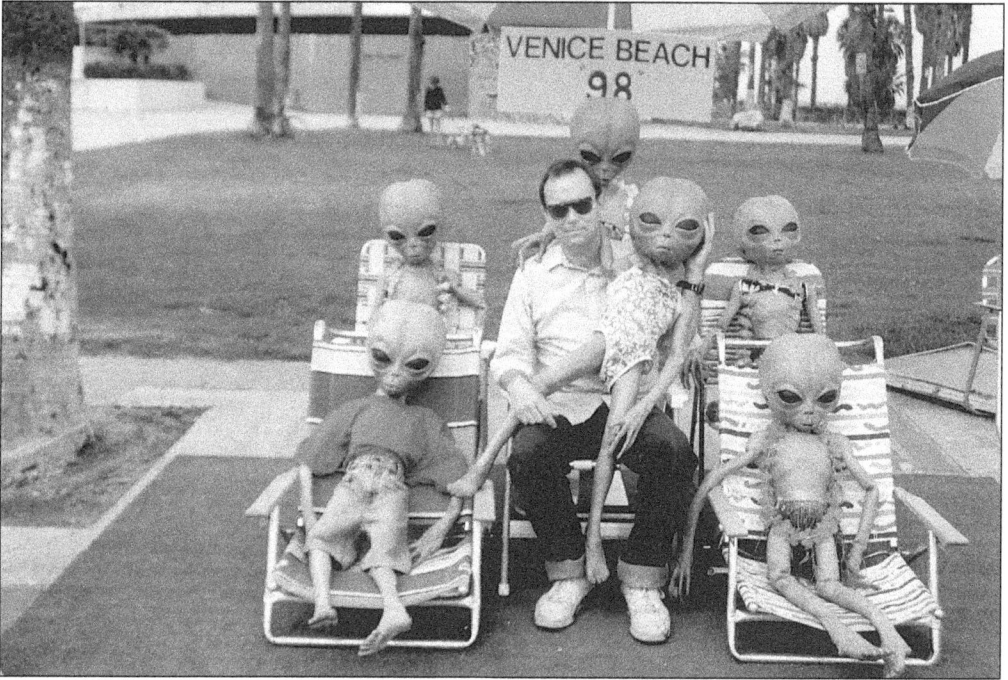

Art F. Palmer seriously communes with faraway visitors to Ocean Front Walk in this cute photo concession. The area in back of this concession was once occupied by the great Abbot Kinney Pier, and later, the even larger 1921 Venice Pier.

Unusually inexpensive price tags on merchandise mingles with unusually high prices here on the oceanfront. The Boardwalk is a colorful carnival of all varieties of humanity. Here, stride pianist Barry "The Lion" Gordon is reflected in a mirror also showing the pristine beach, the Pacific Ocean, and the strand. (Courtesy Schell Alexander.)

The Venice Historical Society leads groups of people all over the city in five different tours. The most unusual is an annual Halloween Walk that begins at the southern canals and ends at the old Grand Lagoon, now a traffic circle. Stops on the tour include murder sites and haunted houses. At left is the author, and Jill Eltrich is at right. (Courtesy Ken Eltrich.)

Another tradition is the annual Canal Christmas Parade staged by residents of the waterways. This couple has decorated the bow of their boat to resemble a Christmas tree. Because it was top heavy, the craft capsized before the end of the parade route.

The annual Kite Festival was a Venice tradition that has recently been revived. Contestants for prizes can choose between homemade kites or a prefabricated model. In a 1980s event, one kite entered had over 100 colorful pieces flying in the ocean breeze.

A Grand Canal bridge was replaced by a new and more picturesque span. Oily, odorous water once flowed in this waterway on the oil-derricked peninsula, where actor Orson Wells "died" at the climax of his riveting 1950s movie, *A Touch of Evil.*

The decaying canals were deemed dangerous with crumbling banks, trash scattered on walkways, and vegetation growing untrammeled. The Fish and Game Department declared the ducks diseased, rounded up the flocks they could find, and euthanized them. Residents hid favorite fowl and released them to other waterways.

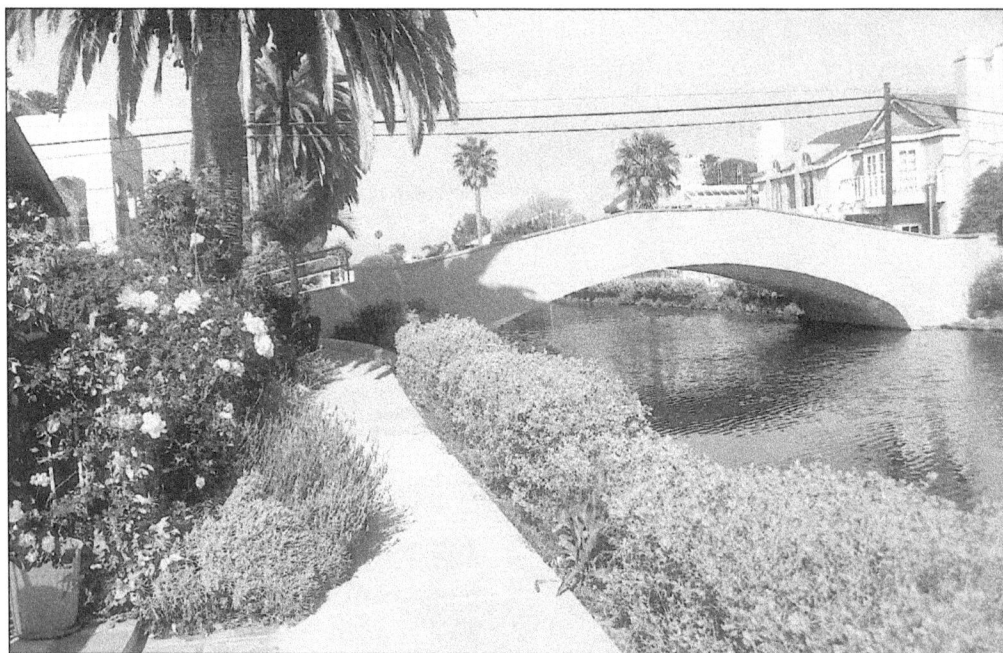

The channels were finally drained and cleaned of toxic mud. A pumping system was installed under the ground, and the tidal gates were replaced with more modern technology. On opening day, Councilwoman Ruth Galanter cut the ribbon with giant scissors, making the canals accessible to boaters and swimmers.

A woolly fog settles over the ethereal canals at daybreak, making the channels appear spectral and surreal. The water is still. Ghostly ducks, and perhaps their ancestors of 80 years ago, glide past without breaking the spell of silence.

You can close your eyes and almost hear the splashing of canoe paddles, the excited voices of children, and the chugging of ancient motorcars as they navigate the arched canal bridges—from a century already gone by.

ABOUT THE AUTHOR

Carolyn Elayne Alexander was born in Harrisburg, Pennsylvania, and is of both Irish and Swiss Mennonite heritage. She arrived in California in 1968 and began rollerskating in Venice a year later. She considered the town's architecture fascinating and tried to discover why it was so unusual. When Tom Moran and Tom Sewell wrote *Fantasy By the Sea*, she walked around Venice comparing historic photographs to the modern street, trying to find remains of the original city. The results were distressing.

It was not until 1984 that Elayne became deeply involved in Venice history, when a group of genealogists conceived the idea of writing a book as a public service project. That book, *Abbot Kinney's Venice-of-America, Volume I*, was penned by Elayne and published in 1992. It was followed by a biography, *On the Wings of an Eagle*, concerning one of the city's pioneers, in 1995. She is the author of five books (three on Venice) with two more in progress: Volume II of the 1992 trilogy and a Pennsylvania Dutch cookbook.

As a photographer, writer, and producer of sound-recorded, historic, tape-slide shows, Ms. Alexander has won two worldwide first-place prizes in slide show competitions and has been officially recognized by the city of Los Angeles for *Goodbye God*, a history of Bodie, California.

In 1994, Elayne was given an Individual Award of Merit and honored by the California Conference of Historical Societies for her work in Venice. She currently serves as president of the Venice Historical Society and gives five different two-hour historic walking tours of the city.

128

www.ingramcontent.com/pod-product-compliance
Lightning Source LLC
Chambersburg PA
CBHW050606110426
42813CB00008B/2474